SPANISH J 641.36 BEN
Benduhn, Tea.
Meat and beans = Carne y
legumbres / Tea Benduhn.

FIND OUT ABOUT **FOOD**
CONOCE LA **COMIDA**

MEAT AND BEANS / CARNE Y LEGUMBRES

by/por Tea Benduhn

Reading consultant/Consultora de lectura: Susan Nations, M.Ed., author, literacy coach, consultant in literacy development/ autora, tutora de alfabetización, consultora de desarrollo de la lectura

WEEKLY READER®
PUBLISHING

Please visit our web site at: www.garethstevens.com
For a free color catalog describing our list of high-quality books,
call 1-800-542-2595 (USA) or 1-800-387-3178 (Canada).

Library of Congress Cataloging-in-Publication Data available upon request from publisher.

ISBN: 978-0-8368-8456-2 (lib. bdg.)
ISBN: 978-0-8368-8463-0 (softcover)

This edition first published in 2008 by
Weekly Reader® Books
An imprint of Gareth Stevens Publishing
1 Reader's Digest Road
Pleasantville, NY 10570-7000 USA

Copyright © 2008 by Gareth Stevens, Inc.

Managing editor: Valerie J. Weber
Art direction: Tammy West
Graphic designer: Scott Krall
Picture research: Diane Laska-Swanke
Photographer: Gregg Andersen
Production: Jessica Yanke
Spanish translation: Tatiana Acosta and Guillermo Gutiérrez

All rights reserved. No part of this book may be reproduced, stored in a retrieval system, or transmitted in any form or by any means, electronic, mechanical, photocopying, recording, or otherwise, without the prior written permission of the copyright holder.

Printed in the United States of America

1 2 3 4 5 6 7 8 9 11 10 09 08 07

Note to Educators and Parents

Reading is such an exciting adventure for young children! They are beginning to integrate their oral language skills with written language. To encourage children along the path to early literacy, books must be colorful, engaging, and interesting; they should invite the young reader to explore both the print and the pictures.

The *Find Out About Food* series is designed to help children understand the value of good nutrition and eating to stay healthy. In each book, young readers will learn how their favorite foods — and possibly some new ones — fit into a balanced diet.

Each book is specially designed to support the young reader in the reading process. The familiar topics are appealing to young children and invite them to read — and re-read — again and again. The full-color photographs and enhanced text further support the student during the reading process.

In addition to serving as wonderful picture books in schools, libraries, homes, and other places where children learn to love reading, these books are specifically intended to be read within an instructional guided reading group. This small group setting allows beginning readers to work with a fluent adult model as they make meaning from the text. After children develop fluency with the text and content, the book can be read independently. Children and adults alike will find these books supportive, engaging, and fun!

— Susan Nations, M.Ed., author, literacy coach, and consultant in literacy development

Nota para los maestros y los padres

¡Leer es una aventura tan emocionante para los niños pequeños! A esta edad están comenzando a integrar su manejo del lenguaje oral con el lenguaje escrito. Para animar a los niños en el camino de la lectura incipiente, los libros deben ser coloridos, estimulantes e interesantes; deben invitar a los jóvenes lectores a explorar la letra impresa y las ilustraciones.

Conoce la comida es una colección diseñada para ayudar a los jóvenes lectores a entender la importancia de una nutrición apropiada y el papel de la alimentación en la salud. En cada libro, los jóvenes lectores aprenderán de qué forma sus alimentos favoritos —y posiblemente algunos nuevos— pueden formar parte de una dieta balanceada.

Cada libro está especialmente diseñado para ayudar a los jóvenes lectores en el proceso de lectura. Los temas familiares llaman la atención de los niños y los invitan a leer una y otra vez. Las fotografías a todo color y el tamaño de la letra ayudan aún más al estudiante en el proceso de lectura.

Además de servir como maravillosos libros ilustrados en escuelas, bibliotecas, hogares y otros lugares donde los niños aprenden a amar la lectura, estos libros han sido especialmente concebidos para ser leídos en un grupo de lectura guiada. Este contexto permite que los lectores incipientes trabajen con un adulto que domina la lectura mientras van determinando el significado del texto. Una vez que los niños dominan el texto y el contenido, el libro puede ser leído de manera independiente. ¡Estos libros les resultarán útiles, estimulantes y divertidos a niños y a adultos por igual!

— Susan Nations, M.Ed., autora, tutora de alfabetización, consultora de desarrollo de la lectura

Do you like to eat chicken or **lentils**? Chicken is a type of meat. Lentils are a type of bean.

¿Te gusta comer pollo o **lentejas**? El pollo es un tipo de carne. Las lentejas son un tipo de legumbre.

Meat and beans are part of the **food pyramid**. The six colored bands on the food pyramid stand for types of foods. Make smart choices. Eat these foods and **exercise** every day.

La carne y las legumbres son parte de la **pirámide alimentaria**. Cada una de las seis franjas de colores de la pirámide representa un tipo de alimento. Elige de forma inteligente. Consume estos alimentos y haz **ejercicio** todos los días.

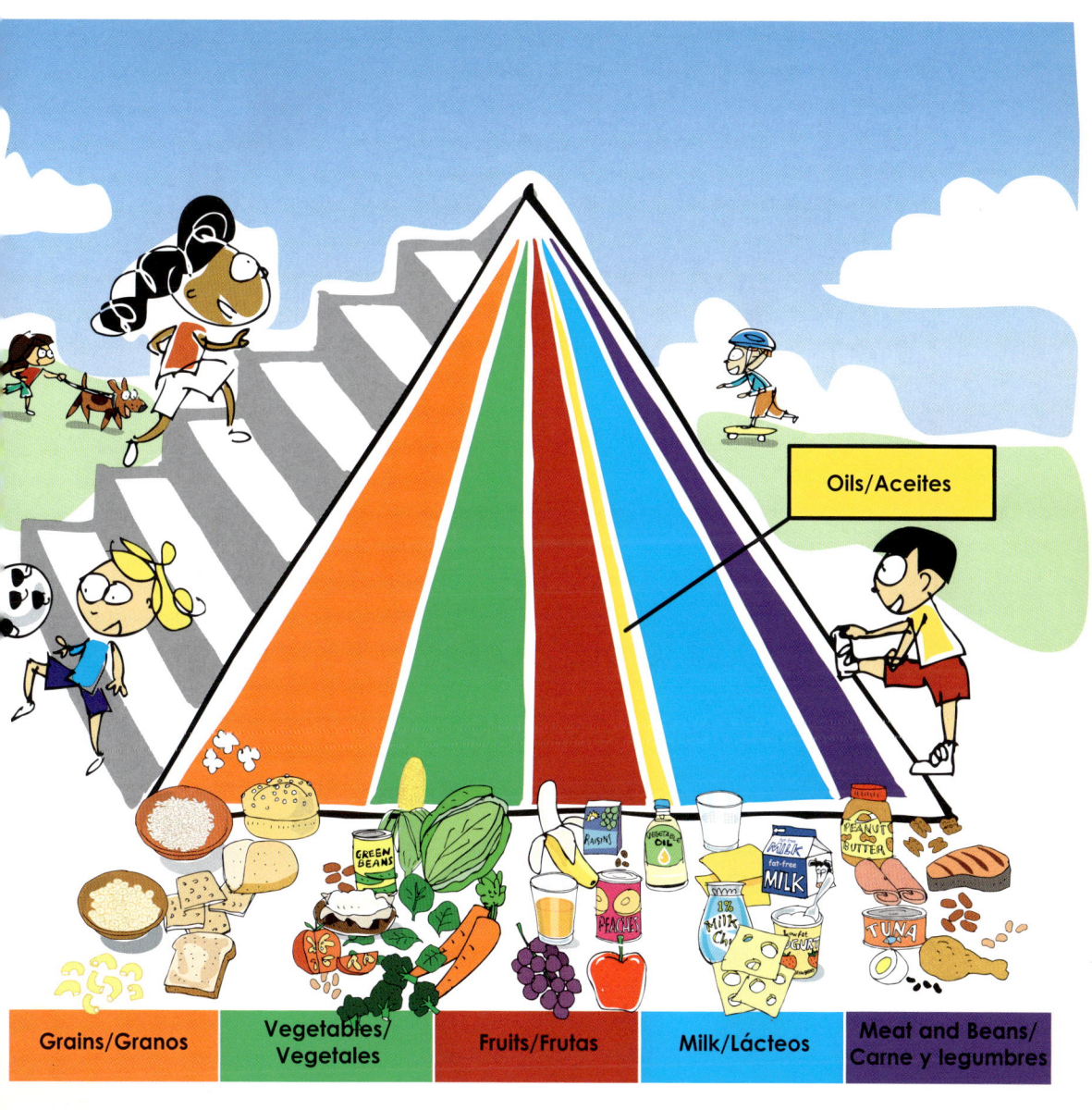

The purple band stands for meat and beans. It is thinner than most of the other bands. You should eat small amounts of meat or beans every day.

La franja morada representa la carne y las legumbres. Esta franja es más delgada que casi todas las demás. A diario, se debe comer una pequeña cantidad de carne o legumbres.

Meat and beans are good for you. They have **protein**. Protein makes your **muscles** strong.

Comer carne y legumbres es bueno. Tienen **proteínas.** Las proteínas ayudan a fortalecer los **músculos**.

Meat and beans have **iron**, too. Iron gives you **energy**.

La carne y las legumbres también tienen **hierro**.
El hierro te da **energía**.

You can eat lots of different kinds of meat, fish, and beans. Try some trout. Chili with pinto beans tastes good, too.

Puedes comer carne, pescado y legumbres de muchos tipos diferentes. Prueba la trucha. El guiso de frijoles pintos también está muy rico.

Some people do not eat meat. They eat many kinds of beans instead. Pea soup provides protein.

Algunas personas no comen carne. En su lugar, comen legumbres de muchos tipos. La sopa de chícharos proporciona proteínas.

Nuts and seeds are also in the meat and beans group. They provide protein, too. Peanuts are seeds. Peanut butter is made from peanuts.

Las nueces y las semillas también están en el grupo de la carne y las legumbres. También proporcionan proteínas. Los cacahuates son semillas. La mantequilla de cacahuate se hace con cacahuates.

Even eggs fit in this food group. They have protein, too. What kinds of eggs, meat, nuts, or beans are you hungry for?

Hasta los huevos pertenecen a este grupo de alimentos. Los huevos también tienen proteínas. ¿Qué platillo con huevos, carne, nueces o frijoles te apetecería comer?

21

Glossary/Glosario

food pyramid — the drawing that shows six colored bands that stand for the six different food groups people should eat every day

healthy — strong and free from illness

iron — a part of certain kinds of foods that help your blood stay healthy

protein — a part of certain kinds of foods that help your body grow and build muscles

trout — a type of fish

---

hierro — mineral que contienen algunos alimentos y que ayuda al buen estado de la sangre

pirámide alimentaria — dibujo que muestra seis franjas de colores que representan seis grupos diferentes de alimentos que las personas deben comer a diario

proteína — parte de ciertos tipos de alimentos que ayuda al crecimiento y a la formación de los músculos

saludable — fuerte y sin enfermedades

trucha — tipo de pescado

For More Information/Más información

Books/Libros

Las carnes y las proteínas. Las grupos de alimentos (series). Robin Nelson (Lerner Publications)

The Meat and Protein Group. The Food Guide Pyramid (series). Helen Frost (Capstone Press)

Meats and Protein. Food Groups (series). Jill Kalz (Smart Apple Media)

Web Sites/Páginas Web

My Pyramid for Kids
mypyramid.gov/kids/index.html
Click on links to play a game and learn more at the government's Web site about the food pyramid.

Publisher's note to educators and parents: Our editors have carefully reviewed this Web site to ensure that it is suitable for children. Many Web sites change frequently, however, and we cannot guarantee that a site's future contents will continue to meet our high standards of quality and educational value. Be advised that children should be closely supervised whenever they access the Internet.

Index/Índice

chicken 4
chili 14
eggs 20
energy 12
exercise 6
food pyramid 6
iron 12
lentils 4
muscles 10
nuts 18, 20
pea soup 16
peanut butter 18
pinto beans 14

protein 10, 16, 18, 20
seeds 18
trout 14

— — — — —

ejercicio 6
energía 12
frijoles pintos 14
guiso de frijoles 14
hierro 12
huevos 20
lentejas 4

mantequilla de cacahuate 18
músculos 10
nueces 18, 20
pirámide alimentaria 6
pollo 4
proteínas 10, 16, 18, 20
semillas 18
sopa de chícharos 16
trucha 14

About the Author/Información sobre la autora

Tea Benduhn writes and edits books for children and teens. She lives in the beautiful state of Wisconsin with her husband and two cats. The walls of their home are lined with bookshelves filled with books. Tea says, "I read every day. It is more fun than watching television!"

Tea Benduhn escribe y corrige libros para niños y adolescentes. Vive en el bello estado de Wisconsin con su esposo y dos gatos. Las paredes de su casa están cubiertas de estanterías con libros. Tea dice: "Leo todos los días. ¡Es más divertido que ver televisión!".